Heinemann First
ENCYCLOPEDIA

Volume 11
Squ-Tur

Heinemann Library
Chicago, Illinois

© 1999, 2006 Heinemann Library
a division of Reed Elsevier Inc.
Chicago, Illinois

Customer Service   888–454–2279

Visit our website at www.heinemannlibrary.com

Series Editors: Rebecca and Stephen Vickers, Gianna Williams
Author Team: Rob Alcraft, Catherine Chambers, Sabrina Crewe, Jim Drake, Fred Martin, Angela Royston, Jane Shuter, Roger Thomas, Rebecca Vickers, Stephen Vickers

This revised and expanded edition produced for Heinemann Library by Discovery Books.
Photo research by Katherine Smith and Rachel Tisdale
Designed by Keith Williams, Michelle Lisseter, and Gecko
Illustrations by Stefan Chabluk and Mark Bergin

Originated by Ambassador Litho Limited
Printed in China by WKT Company Limited

10 09 08 07 06
10 9 8 7 6 5 4 3 2

Library of Congress Cataloging-in-Publication Data

Heinemann first encyclopedia.
        p.   cm.
    Summary: A fourteen-volume encyclopedia covering animals, plants, countries, transportation, science, ancient civilizations, US states, US presidents, and world history
        ISBN 1-4034-7118-5 (v. 11 : lib. bdg.)
    1. Children's encyclopedias and dictionaries.
    I. Heinemann Library (Firm)
    AG5.H45 2005
    031—dc22   2005006176

Acknowledgments
Cover: Cover photographs of a desert, an electric guitar, a speedboat, an iceberg, a man on a camel, cactus flowers, and the Colosseum at night reproduced with permission of Corbis. Cover photograph of the Taj Mahal reproduced with permission of Digital Stock. Cover photograph of an x-ray of a man reproduced with permission of Digital Vision. Cover photographs of a giraffe, the Leaning Tower of Pisa, the Statue of Liberty, a white owl, a cactus, a butterfly, a saxophone, an astronaut, cars at night, and a circuit board reproduced with permission of Getty Images/Photodisc. Cover photograph of Raglan Castle reproduced with permission of Peter Evans; J. Allan Cash Ltd., pp. 6, 12 top, 16 bottom, 17, 20, 21, 22, 23, 30, 41 bottom, 43, 44 bottom, 46 top, 48; Ancient Art and Architecture, p. 13 bottom; Bettman/Corbis, p. 10 bottom; Brian Wilson, p. 13 top; Trevor Clifford Photography, pp. 12 bottom, 24 bottom; BBC Natural History Unit/Jeff Foott, p. 37 bottom; Hulton Getty, pp. 40 top, 44 top; The Hutchison Library, Andrew Hill, p. 31 top; Niall Benvie, p. 5 top; C. Borland/PhotoLink, p. 27; Pat Clay, p. 34 bottom; J.A.L. Cooke, p. 28 right; E.R. Degginer, p. 5 bottom; Jack Dermid, p. 34 top; Fredrik Ehrenstrom, p. 9 top; Evans/Three Lions/Getty Images, p. 8 top; Sally and Richard Greenhill, p. 14 bottom; Kent Knudson/ PhotoLink, p. 29; Chris Kapolka, p. 39 top; Martin Koretz, p. 40 bottom; Richard Kolar, p. 33 bottom; Lon E. Lauber, p. 46 bottom; Pat and Tom Leeson, p. 19 bottom; Tom McHugh, p. 4 top; Andrew J. Martinez, p. 4 bottom; MPI/Getty Images, p. 45; NASA/Warren Faidley, p. 7 bottom; Rob Nunnington, p. 28 left; Reuters/Mike Segar, p. 8 bottom; Kjell Sandved, p. 9 bottom; Frank Schneidermeyer, p. 32 bottom; Tony Tilford, p. 19 top; Redferns/Mick Hutson, p. 15 bottom; Science Photo Library/BSIP-LECA, p. 38 bottom; Science Photo Library/ESA, p. 18 bottom; Library of Congress, p. 25 bottom; Francoise Sauze, p. 25 top; Shakespeare's Globe/John Tramper, p. 31 bottom; Tony Stone Images/John Elk, p. 15 top; Tony Stone Worldwide, p. 47; David Sams, p. 36; PhotoDisc, p. 10 top.

Every effort has been made to contact copyright holders of any material reproduced in this book. Any omissions will be rectified in subsequent printings if notice is given to the Publisher.

Welcome to
Heinemann First Encyclopedia

What is an encyclopedia?

An encyclopedia is an information book. It gives the most important facts about many different subjects. This encyclopedia has been written for children who are using an encyclopedia for the first time. It covers many of the subjects from school and others you may find interesting.

What is in this encyclopedia?

In this encyclopedia, each topic is called an *entry*. There is one page of information for every entry. The entries in this encyclopedia explain

- animals
- plants
- dinosaurs
- countries
- geography
- history
- world religions
- music
- art
- transportation
- science
- technology
- states
- famous Americans

How to use this encyclopedia

This encyclopedia has thirteen books called *volumes*. The first twelve volumes contain entries. The entries are all in alphabetical order. This means that Volume 1 starts with entries that begin with the letter A and Volume 12 ends with entries that begin with the letter Z. Volume 13 is the index volume. It also has other interesting information.

Here are two entries that show you what you can find on a page:

The "see also" line tells you where to find other related information.

This is the letter that the entry starts with.

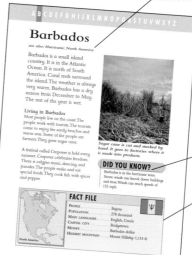

Did You Know? boxes have fun or interesting bits of information.

Fact boxes give you details about the topic.

The Fact File tells you important facts and figures.

Squid

see also: Mollusk, Sea Life

A squid is a type of mollusk. It is an invertebrate. Squid live mostly in warm seas. Some squid are tiny. Other squid are very large. The squid squirts a black liquid called ink at its enemies. The ink blinds the enemies. Then the squid escapes.

SQUID FACTS

NUMBER OF KINDS	more than 300
COLOR	can change color
LENGTH	up to 50 feet
STATUS	common
LIFE SPAN	2 to 5 years
ENEMIES	fish, seals, whales, people

Squid families

Most squid get together in large groups to mate. These groups are called shoals. The female squid lays about 2,000 eggs. She sticks the eggs to seaweed or rocks. The baby squid hatch after three or four weeks. They take care of themselves. Squid are fully grown in two years.

a shell under the skin for extra protection

large eyes to see under the sea

ten tentacles with suckers for catching food

a Californian market squid

These long-finned squid and a newly-laid mass of eggs are on the bottom of the sea.

MEAT EATER

A squid eats mostly fish and animals with shells. It catches a fish by holding it with its long tentacles. Then it paralyzes the fish with a special poison.

Squirrel

see also: Mammal

A squirrel is a small mammal. It has a bushy tail. Squirrels have large eyes. They have strong legs and claws. They have big front teeth for nibbling tree bark and nuts. Squirrels live in most parts of the world.

SQUIRREL FACTS

NUMBER OF KINDS	more than 70
COLOR	red, brown, gray, beige
LENGTH	5 inches to 3 feet
WEIGHT	less than an ounce to 18 lbs.
STATUS	common
LIFE SPAN	2 to 10 years
ENEMIES	birds of prey, foxes, people

bushy tail for balance while running and jumping

a red squirrel

big front teeth for nibbling food

paws for gripping food

Squirrel families

A female squirrel has several babies at a time. Both parents and the babies live in a nest built by the parents.

There are many different kinds of squirrels. Red and gray squirrels live in trees. The flying squirrel has big flaps of skin that it can hold open. It glides from tree to tree. Ground squirrels and prairie dogs live in holes or underground burrows.

PLANT AND INSECT EATER

Squirrels eat bark, nuts, mushrooms, seeds, and some insects. They hide food to eat in the winter.

These baby gray squirrels will be looked after by both parents until they are older.

Sri Lanka

see also: Asia

Sri Lanka is a country in south Asia. It is made up of one big island and some smaller islands. The north has flat land. There are mountains in the center of the big island. The areas of lower ground are hot and wet.

Living in Sri Lanka

Most people in Sri Lanka live in the country. They grow rice, coconuts, rubber trees, and tea. They often cook their rice with mango, coconut, and peanuts. Coconuts, cloves, and cinnamon are used to flavor bean, meat, and fish dishes. Sri Lankans in the cities make chemicals and building materials.

Sri Lankan dancing is well-known. Each small dance movement has a meaning. There is a lot of dancing at the *Perahara* festival. This is a torchlight parade with decorated elephants.

This woman is doing a dance called Kandyan *dance. It is named after the city of Kandy. The* Kandyan *dance is the national dance-drama of Sri Lanka.*

DID YOU KNOW?

Sri Lanka was called Ceylon until 1972.

Asia

FACT FILE

PEOPLE	Sri Lankans
POPULATION	almost 20 million
MAIN LANGUAGES	Sinhala, Tamil, English
CAPITAL CITY	Colombo
MONEY	Sri Lankan rupee
HIGHEST MOUNTAIN	Pidurutalagala—8,284 feet
LONGEST RIVER	Mahaweli Ganga—130 miles

Star

see also: Solar System, Sun

Stars are huge balls of burning gas. The sun is the star at the center of our solar system. Other stars look smaller because they are so far away. It takes years for the light of stars to reach Earth. Some stars are much bigger than our sun.

The night sky

Thousands of stars can be seen in the night sky. Some stars look brighter than others. Some stars also seem to be different colors. Bluish stars are the hottest. Yellow stars are the coolest.

Distances between stars are often measured in the number of years it takes the light to reach Earth. One light-year is how far light travels in one year. The stars nearest the earth are about four light-years away. This is about 25 trillion miles.

The Andromeda galaxy has millions of stars.

> ## DID YOU KNOW?
> People have always seen patterns in the stars in the night skies. These patterns are called constellations. Many are named after heroes and gods from ancient times.

1. A star begins as a large cloud of gases.

2. The star becomes smaller and hotter. It begins to shine.

3. The star burns up over thousands of millions of years. It swells into a red giant.

4. The star may explode and end as a white dwarf.

stages in the life of a star

Star-Spangled Banner

see also: American Flag, Flag

"The Star-Spangled Banner" is the national anthem of the United States of America. A national anthem is a nation's official song. It is a symbol for that country.

This is a portrait of Francis Scott Key, who wrote the words to the song.

A patriot's poem

In 1814, the United States was fighting Britain in the War of 1812. A battle was fought at Fort McHenry, a fort in Baltimore, Maryland. Francis Scott Key was a lawyer who had joined the fight against the British. He watched the battle from a nearby ship.

Key worried that the Americans inside Fort McHenry had been defeated. But the morning after the battle, he saw the American flag still flying over the fort. Key wrote a poem about the event. He named it "The Defense of Fort McHenry."

DID YOU KNOW?

The United States has other patriotic songs. "Hail to the Chief" is played to announce the president. "America the Beautiful" is sung at many occasions. So is "America" (also known as "My Country 'Tis of Thee").

A national anthem

After the Americans defeated the British, Key's poem became famous. It was set to music. The music was originally for another song called "Anacreon in Heaven." Everyone called the new song "The Star-Spangled Banner." Soldiers liked to sing it during the Civil War. In 1916, President Woodrow Wilson said "The Star-Spangled Banner" should be played at official occasions. The song became the national anthem in 1931.

Fans hold up a flag at Giants Stadium as they sing the national anthem.

Starfish

see also: Invertebrate, Sea Life

A starfish is a sea animal. It is star-shaped and has five legs. Its skin is bony and hard. Starfish live in seas all over the world.

Starfish families

Starfish babies come from millions of tiny eggs. The starfish floats these eggs out into the sea. The eggs settle in rock pools. They hatch into tiny rectangular larvae. The larvae float about in the sea until they grow into adult starfish.

STARFISH FACTS

NUMBER OF KINDS	1,600
COLOR	all colors
LENGTH	less than a half inch to 3 feet
STATUS	common
LIFE SPAN	about 6 years
ENEMIES	fish, other starfish

suckers on each foot to grip rocks and food

strong, bendable legs to hold food

eyes at the end of each leg see only light and dark

mouth in the center of the underside

a common starfish

A starfish can grow back lost parts of its body. This single leg is growing another complete body.

MEAT EATER

Starfish are hunters. They eat mussels and sea animals with shells. A starfish wraps its arms around its food. It slowly pulls the shell open. Then it pushes its stomach into the shell and begins to eat.

Statue of Liberty

see also: New York

The Statue of Liberty is a huge sculpture of a woman. Liberty is another word for freedom. The Statue of Liberty is a symbol of freedom. It stands for the freedom of life in the United States of America.

A gift from France

The Statue of Liberty was given to the United States by France. The gift represented the friendship between the two countries. French soldiers fought for Americans in the American Revolution. The Statue of Liberty symbolized America's freedom from Britain after the Revolution.

The Statue of Liberty is in New York Harbor.

The Statue of Liberty arrived from France in 1885. It was in 350 pieces. It was mounted on Liberty Island in New York Harbor.

A symbol of hope

The Statue of Liberty came to symbolize another freedom. Many immigrants came to the United States in the 1800s and 1900s. Most came to escape poverty or prejudice in their own countries. They arrived on ships in New York Harbor. The first thing they saw was the Statue of Liberty. The statue gave them hope.

The Statue of Liberty is often used to represent the United States in political cartoons.

DID YOU KNOW?

The Statue of Liberty is made of copper and steel. She is 151 feet high. She holds a burning torch to represent freedom. The seven spikes of her crown symbolize seven seas and seven continents.

Stegosaurus

see also: Dinosaur, Fossil

A stegosaurus was a four-legged dinosaur. It had big, bony plates sticking up along its back. Its tail had long spikes. The stegosaurus was about ten feet high. It was about as heavy as a rhinoceros.

Lifestyle

The stegosaurus's big, bony plates may have helped it keep the correct body temperature. Plates turned toward the sun would help the stegosaurus soak up the sun's rays. This would warm the stegosaurus. Plates turned away from the sun would help it cool down.

STEGOSAURUS FACTS

LENGTH ... about 30 feet

WEIGHT ... about 2 tons

ENEMIES ... big meat-eating dinosaurs, such as the allosaurus

PLANT EATER

The stegosaurus only ate plants. It had a small, beaklike mouth. It could eat plants from the ground. It may have also stood on its back legs to reach branches.

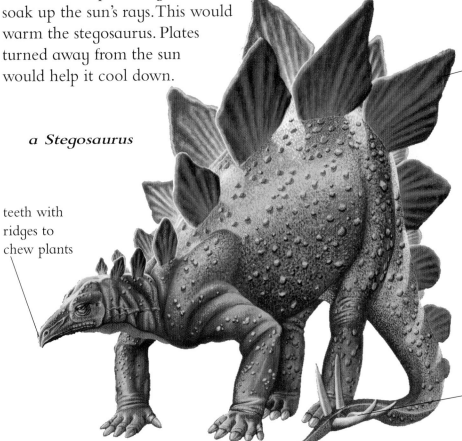

a Stegosaurus

teeth with ridges to chew plants

bony plates for defense and to control body temperature

spikes on tail to fend off enemy attacks

Stem

see also: Plant

A stem is a part of a plant. Leaves and flowers grow from plant stems. The stem carries water from the roots to the leaves. It takes food made in the leaves to the rest of the plant.

How a stem grows

Most stems grow above the ground. The main stem pushes up from the seed through the soil. Sometimes the main stem splits into thinner branch stems. Some plants have underground stems. They form thick, swollen ends called bulbs or tubers. Tulips, daffodils, and crocuses all grow from bulbs. Potatoes are tubers.

Bamboo is the fastest-growing plant. Its stems can grow almost three feet in a day. Some people use the stems of bamboo to build houses and furniture.

People eat the main stems of asparagus and celery. Potatoes and onions are swollen underground stems.

Stone Age

see also: Bronze Age, Iron Age

The Stone Age is the time in history when people made tools and weapons from stone. It is the earliest time in the history of people. The Stone Age began and ended at different times in different places. In Europe, the Stone Age lasted more than two million years.

Why was the Stone Age important?

The Stone Age was important because it was when the first people on Earth found out how to live and work together. Stone Age people learned how to speak. They found out how to use fire to keep warm and to cook food. They started to sew animal skins together to make clothes. They began to paint pictures on walls.

KEY DATES

2,000,000 B.C.	People begin to use stone tools.
1,500,000 B.C.	The first stone axes are made.
75,000 B.C.	People begin to use fire.
20,000 B.C.	People begin to use bows and arrows. They make bone needles and sew skins to make clothes. They draw paintings in caves.
6000 B.C.	People in the Middle East begin to use copper. Their Stone Age ends.

This flint spearhead was made about 6,500 years ago. Tiny pieces of flint were chipped off to get the right shape.

What came next?

Stone tools and weapons took a long time to make. They could break easily. It was not always easy to find the right sort of stone. A hard stone called flint made the best tools. Stone Age people turned to metal for tools and weapons. The first metal they learned to use was copper.

This Stone Age axe head is made of polished flint.

Story

see also: Fable, Fairy Tale, Legend,
Literature, Myth

A story is a way of telling
people about a series of events.
A made up story is called
fiction. A story about true events
is called nonfiction. Stories can
be written down or spoken
from memory. People who
write stories are called authors.
Some stories are put into books.
Some of these books may have
pictures drawn by illustrators.

What is a story?

True and made up stories usually have a
plot. A plot is made up of the beginning,
middle, and end of the story. It also has
characters. Characters are the people
or animals that take part in the story.
All stories have settings. The setting is
the time and place of the story's events.

This is a picture from a story called
Gulliver's Travels. *It is about a man
who visits many unusual places.*

Kinds of stories

Fiction stories have many different
settings. Fantasy stories are set in times
and places that are made up. Fantasies
might include magic, too. Historical
fiction stories are set in the past.
Science fiction is often set in the future.

Mystery and detective stories have
a crime or mystery for the characters
to solve.

*Reading aloud from a book is a
popular way to share a story.*

Stringed Instrument

see also: Music, Musical Instrument, Orchestra

Stringed instruments are musical instruments. They make sounds when strings are plucked, strummed, rubbed, or struck.

The first stringed instruments

The earliest stringed instrument was probably a hunter's bow. It made a "twanging" sound when the string was plucked. The player taps the string with a stick held in one hand. The sound changes by bending the bow and stretching the string.

Types of stringed instruments

Stringed instruments are divided into groups. Bowed string instruments have strings that are rubbed with a bow. The bow has sticky hair. Violins, cellos, and the Indian *sarangi* are bowed instruments.

Plucked string instruments are twanged using the fingers and thumb. Guitars, harps, and the African *kora* are plucked instruments.

Strummed string instruments are brushed with the fingers or with something held in the fingers. Guitars, dulcimers, and ukeleles are strummed instruments.

This Korean man is playing a traditional string instrument called a Koto.

The violin was invented in Europe. It is used in the music of many countries. This is the violinist Vanessa-Mae.

DID YOU KNOW?

One type of bass guitar has strings made from a kind of artificial rubber.

Submarine

see also: Ship, Transportation

A submarine is a boat that can travel under water. Special tanks filled with air let a submarine float. The submarine sinks when the air is let out of the tanks and replaced with water.

The first submarines

The first submarine was made of wood. It was powered by oars. It was rowed underwater along the Thames River near London, England. Submarines today are built of steel. They are large and powerful, and can stay under water for months.

SUBMARINE FACTS

FIRST SUBMARINE	built in 1620
FIRST HAND-POWERED	1876
FIRST STEAM-POWERED	1880
FIRST GAS/ELECTRIC-POWERED	1890s
FIRST NUCLEAR-POWERED	1954
BIGGEST	Russian *Typhoon* class submarine
GREATEST DEPTH	36,102 feet

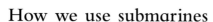

This is an artist's view of the inside of a large military submarine.

How we use submarines

Most submarines are used by navies. Submarines can be used to attack ships and even cities. Smaller submarines called submersibles are used to explore the deep sea and to repair oil rigs.

DID YOU KNOW?

The U.S. nuclear-powered submarine *Nautilus* went under the North Pole in 1958.

Submersibles like this one do scientific work. They can usually carry two or three passengers.

Sudan

see also: Africa

Sudan is a country in northeast Africa. There is desert in the north. There is farm land with hills in the center. There are mountains in the west. Hot, wet swamps and rain forest are in the south. It rains in summer.

These nomads are traveling with all their household goods loaded on a camel.

Living in Sudan

More than half of all Sudanese are farmers. They live in the rural areas and raise animals and grow crops. A common food in Sudan is sorghum and spiced vegetables. Sorghum is an important crop in all the dry areas of Africa. It is a grain that can be grown without much water. Some Sudanese are nomads. They move from place to place looking for food for their animals.

DID YOU KNOW?

Sudan is the largest country in Africa. It is about 1,275 miles from north to south. It is about 1,150 miles from east to west.

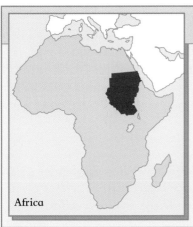

Africa

FACT FILE

PEOPLE	Sudanese
POPULATION	about 39 million
MAIN LANGUAGES	Arabic, African languages
CAPITAL CITY	Khartoum
MONEY	Sudanese Dinar
HIGHEST MOUNTAIN	Mount Kinyeti–10,456 feet
LONGEST RIVER	Nile River–4,145 miles

Sun

see also: Solar System, Star

The sun is the star in the center of the earth's solar system. It is a huge ball of burning gas. It gives out the heat and light that make life on Earth possible. All the planets of the solar system orbit or go around the sun. The planets are held in place by the sun's gravity.

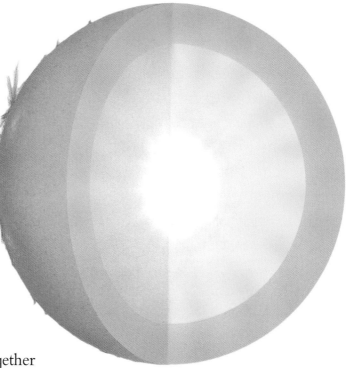

What makes the sun?

The sun is a cloud of gas held together by gravity. The sun has been burning for more than four billion years. It will burn for about another four billion years.

The temperature at the center of the sun is about 27 million degrees. The temperature at the surface is about 10 thousand degrees. There are slightly cooler patches on the sun called sunspots. These look like dark spots on the sun.

STAY SAFE!

A person's eyes can be damaged by looking directly at the sun. Never stare at the sun or look at it with binoculars or a telescope.

Sometimes huge flames up to 62 thousand miles long shoot out of the sun. These flames are called solar flares.

Swan

see also: Bird

Swans are the largest waterbirds in the world. Swans live by lakes, rivers, and canals. Some swans live by the sea. Swans like living in areas where it doesn't get too hot or too cold. Some kinds of swan migrate.

Swan families

A male swan is called a cob. A female swan is called a pen. A baby swan is called a cygnet. A pen and a cob stay together for life. They build a nest on an island, in reeds, or on a beaver lodge. These places make it easier for them to keep enemies away.

The pen lays five or six eggs. She sits on the eggs. The cob brings her food. The cygnets stay with their parents for more than a year.

SWAN FACTS

NUMBER OF KINDS	7
COLOR	white, black, or black and white
LENGTH	up to 6 feet
WEIGHT	up to 26 lbs.
STATUS	common
LIFE SPAN	up to 25 years
ENEMIES	Cygnets may be eaten by foxes and some fish.

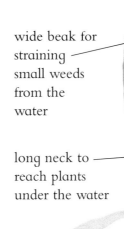

wide beak for straining small weeds from the water

a whooper swan

long neck to reach plants under the water

strong wings to fly a long way

A mother swan keeps her cygnets close when out on the river.

PLANT EATER

A swan eats water plants. Its long neck helps it to reach plants that grow under the water. A swan will also eat grain from the fields.

Sweden

see also: Europe

Sweden is a country in northwest Europe. There are cold, snow-covered mountains in the north. A high, flat area slopes down to the coast. The coast is hilly. Summers are warm. Winters are cold and snowy.

The Swedish royal palace is in Old Stockholm.

Living in Sweden

Most people in Sweden live in cities and large towns. They work in offices and factories. Farmers grow grains and root crops. They raise cows for milk. Fish are caught around the coast. Herring is a favorite fish to eat. There are many forests in the north. The trees are cut for wood. They are also used to make paper.

The Feast of Valborg is held in April. Bonfires are an important part of this Swedish festival.

DID YOU KNOW?

Swedish girls dress up in white dresses at Christmastime. They wear wreaths of candles in their hair. They bring a special breakfast to their parents.

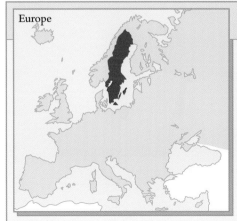

Europe

FACT FILE

PEOPLE	Swedes, Swedish
POPULATION	almost 9 million
MAIN LANGUAGE	Swedish
CAPITAL CITY	Stockholm
MONEY	Swedish krona
HIGHEST MOUNTAIN	Mount Kebnekaise—6,948 feet
LONGEST RIVER	Torne älve—353 miles

Switzerland

see also: Europe

Switzerland is a country in Europe. There are cold, snowy mountains in the south and northwest. There are valleys between the mountains. The valleys have many rivers and lakes. The valleys are warmer and not as wet as the mountains.

Living in Switzerland

Most people in Switzerland live in towns and cities. Switzerland is famous for its watchmakers and clockmakers. Banking is also an important business. Tourists visit Switzerland in the winter to ski. Tourists climb and walk in the summer.

Farmers in Switzerland raise a lot of dairy cattle. The milk is used to make cheeses and chocolates. The Swiss eat many cheeses with different types of bread. They also enjoy eating fried, grated potatoes.

The overhanging roof of this house keeps the snow away from the windows and doors. This style of house is sometimes called a chalet.

DID YOU KNOW?

The word *Helvetia* is on Swiss stamps. This is the name of Celtic people who lived in this area a long time ago.

Europe

FACT FILE

PEOPLE	Swiss
POPULATION	about 7 million
MAIN LANGUAGES	German, French, Italian, Romansch
CAPITAL CITY	Bern
BIGGEST CITY	Zurich
MONEY	Swiss franc
HIGHEST MOUNTAIN	Matterhorn–14,697 feet
LONGEST RIVER	Rhine River–820 miles

Syria

see also: Asia

Syria is a country in the Middle East. There are hills and mountains to the west. High, flat land slopes to a river plain in the east. There are also hot, dry desert areas. It is cooler in the hills. It is warm and wet on the coast.

Living in Syria

About half the people live in towns and cities. There is drilling for oil and mining for phosphates. Food and cloth are made in factories. Syrian farmers grow cotton, grains, olives, beans, and fruit. They also raise sheep, goats, cattle, and donkeys.

Syria is a very old country. Damascus is the oldest city with people still living in it. Today almost all Syrians are followers of Islam.

This is the entrance to a covered market. The market is called a bazaar or a souk.

DID YOU KNOW?

Damask is a kind of patterned fabric that is all one color. It was named after the silks made in Damascus. The silks were taken to Europe hundreds of years ago by traders.

Asia

FACT FILE

PEOPLE	Syrians
POPULATION	about 18 million
MAIN LANGUAGE	Arabic
CAPITAL CITY	Damascus
MONEY	Syrian pound
HIGHEST MOUNTAIN	Jabal ash-Shaykh–9,236 feet
LONGEST RIVER	Euphrates River–1,677 miles

Taiwan

see also: Asia, China

Taiwan is an island country. It is in east Asia. Mountains with forests are in the east. Farm land is in the west. Summers are hot and humid. Winters are mild and wet and may have hurricanes.

The old Royal Palace in Taipei is now a museum.

Living in Taiwan

Most people in Taiwan live in towns and cities. They work in offices and factories. Farmers in the country grow rice, fruit, tea, and soybeans. Fish are caught in the sea around Taiwan. Taiwanese eat dried fish. They fry the fish with peanuts. They also make oyster omelettes.

Almost all of the people in Taiwan are Chinese. They hold ancient Chinese festivals. Boats with dragons' heads are raced in the yearly Dragon Boat Festival.

DID YOU KNOW?

Taiwan is also known as Formosa. Portuguese traders gave it this name in 1590. Formosa means "beautiful one."

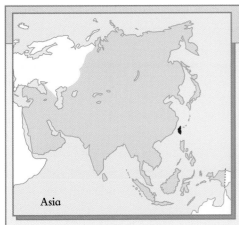

Asia

FACT FILE

PEOPLE	Taiwanese
POPULATION	about 21 million
MAIN LANGUAGES	Mandarin Chinese
CAPITAL CITY	Taipei
MONEY	New Taiwan dollar
HIGHEST MOUNTAIN	Mount Yu Shan—13,118 feet
LONGEST RIVER	Choshui—124 miles

Taste

see also: Smell, Touch

Taste is one of the five senses. The tiny bumps on the tongue are called taste buds. Taste buds tell the brain if something in the mouth is salty, bitter, sweet, or sour. A fifth taste, umami, is when the tongue senses savory food, like meat or cheese.

Tongue areas

Once it was thought that different areas of the tongue sensed different tastes. But now we know that there are only small differences between how one part of the tongue tastes compared to another.

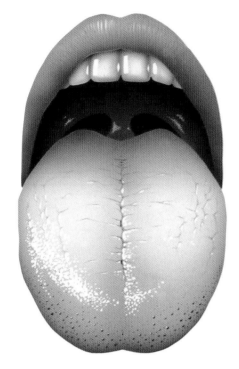

The only part of the tongue that cannot taste is the middle top area.

Bitter

Salty

Sour

Sweet

Different foods have different tastes.

Taste and smell

The sense of taste is helped by the sense of smell. Some foods are given their taste by how they smell. When food is chewed the smell gets into the nose. Most things will taste the same if the nose is pinched closed.

DID YOU KNOW?

Things that taste bitter are sometimes bad to eat. The bitter taste is a warning.

Telephone

see also: Communication

A telephone is a machine that lets people speak to each other when they are not together. People can use a telephone to speak to friends next door. They can even speak to someone on the other side of the world.

The first telephone

The telephone was invented by the Scottish scientist Alexander Graham Bell. He invented it in the United States in 1876. He used an electric current to send and receive the human voice.

This telephone has a case made of clear plastic so the insides can be seen.

Alexander Graham Bell is showing others his telephone invention in 1892.

Telephones today

All telephone calls had to travel along wires until the 1970s. Expensive cables carried telephone messages under the oceans. Now, satellite communication has made long distance telephone calls cheaper. The signals travel up to the satellite and down again by radio waves. New communication methods use the telephone system, too. Fax machines, computer e-mail, and the Internet use the telephone system to send words and pictures instead of voices.

DID YOU KNOW?

Cellular telephones use radio signals. Each cellular telephone has its own little receiver and transmitter for radio waves.

Television

see also: Communication, Radio

A television is a machine. It picks up radio waves and turns them into sounds and pictures. Television is used for entertainment. It also gives information such as news and weather reports.

> ## DID YOU KNOW?
> The first television service began in 1936 in Britain. It was in black and white. Color television began in 1953 in the United States.

The first television

Two systems of television were invented by two different people. The inventors were John Logie Baird and Vladimir Zworykin. At first, all TV shows were broadcast live. There was no way of recording them. The first TV pictures were fuzzy, small, and black and white. Today there are much bigger televisions. The pictures are in color. New wide-screen, digital, and high-definition TVs give bigger and better pictures.

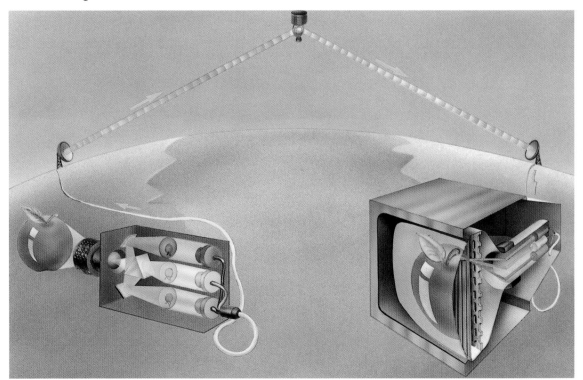

Radio waves are sent to a satellite orbiting the earth. The signal bounces back to the earth.

Tennessee

see also: United States of America

Tennessee is a state in the southern United States of America. It is bordered by eight other states. The land changes from hills to flat farm land to mountains. The Tennessee River crosses the state twice, in the east and in the west. The weather in Tennessee is very warm and humid.

A crop grows tall at the side of a farm shed.

Life in Tennessee

Most people in Tennessee live in cities. Memphis is the largest city in Tennessee. It is a busy port and trading center for the cotton industry.

The capital, Nashville, is the second largest city. It is a center for the country music industry. The famous Country Music Hall of Fame and Museum is in Nashville.

DID YOU KNOW?

The Grand Ole Opry radio program is broadcast out of Nashville. It has been running since 1925. It is the longest-running live radio program in the world.

People in Tennessee's cities work in services and manufacturing. Factory workers make all kinds of goods. Outside of the cities, much of Tennessee is farmland. Tennessee's farmers raise cattle and chickens. They grow cotton, soybeans, and tobacco.

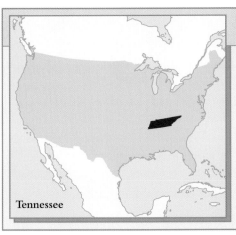

Tennessee

FACT FILE

BECAME A STATE... 1796 (16th state)

LAND AREA......... 41,217 square miles
(34th largest land area)

POPULATION 5,841,748
(16th most populated state)

OTHER NAME ...... Volunteer State

CAPITAL CITY ...... Nashville

Termite

see also: Insect

A termite is an insect. It is small and blind. Groups of termites build very large nests. Termites live all around the world. They live mainly in warm countries.

Termite families

Termites live in big groups called colonies. Two termites with wings fly from one colony to start a new colony. These two termites are called the king and the queen. They build a new, small nest. The queen grows larger. She lays as many as 30 thousand eggs each day. Most of these eggs hatch as worker termites. They help to bring up the young. They make the nest bigger and bigger. Some of the eggs hatch as soldier termites. They protect the nest.

TERMITE FACTS

NUMBER OF KINDS	2,300
COLOR	brown or white
LENGTH	queen–up to 5 inches; soldier–less than 1 inch
STATUS	common
LIFE SPAN	kings and queens live up to 10 years
ENEMIES	anteaters, pangolins, aardvarks, people

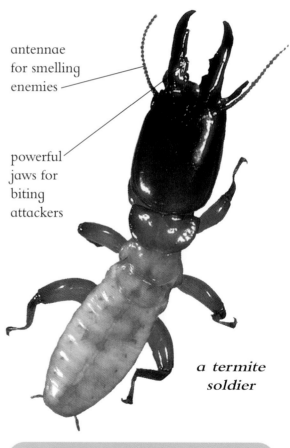

antennae for smelling enemies

powerful jaws for biting attackers

a termite soldier

This huge mound was built by millions of tiny termites.

PLANT EATER

A termite eats wood. Its stomach is very good at digesting wood.

Texas

see also: Bush, George W.; United States of America

Texas is a state in the southern United States of America. It is very big. Much of the land is flat grassland, but there are mountains and hills, too. There are miles of coast along the Gulf of Mexico. Most of Texas is very hot. Some parts are dry. The climate is humid near the coast.

Life in Texas

Texas is rich in natural resources of many kinds. Its main resource is oil. Many people in Texas work in the oil industry.

Farming is an important industry in the state. Ranchers in Texas raise the most cattle and sheep in the United States. The state grows more cotton than any other state.

Oil pumps are a familiar sight in Texas.

DID YOU KNOW?

Texas is the only state that has been ruled by six nations. They are Spain, France, Mexico, the Republic of Texas, the United States of America, and—during the Civil War—the Confederate States of America.

Texas is also an important manufacturing state. Workers in factories process the state's natural resources. They refine oil and make chemicals. Some factories make clothes from cotton and wool. Others process and pack foods.

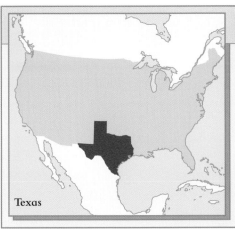

Texas

FACT FILE

BECAME A STATE	1845 (28th state)
LAND AREA	261,797 square miles (2nd largest land area)
POPULATION	22,118,509 (2nd most populated state)
OTHER NAME	Lone Star State
CAPITAL CITY	Austin

Thailand

see also: Asia

Thailand is a country in southeast Asia. There are mountains in the north. There is high, flat land in the east. Wide rivers flow through the center. Forests cover about one-third of Thailand. The weather is mostly hot. There is a dry season and a very wet season.

Living in Thailand

Most people work on small farms. They grow rice, vegetables, cassava, corn, and cotton. Some of the rice is sold to other countries. There are not many factories. Tourists visit Thailand. They enjoy the beautiful beaches, Thai food, dancing, and music. Most Thai food is cooked with spices, chilies, and peppers. The food is very hot and spicy.

Most people in Thailand are Buddhists. There are thousands of Buddhist shrines and temples.

Thai dancers wear costumes that are like the costumes worn hundreds of years ago.

DID YOU KNOW?

Some farmers use buffaloes to pull plows in the rice fields.

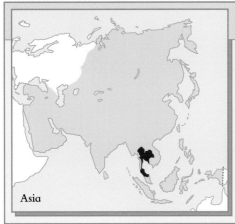

Asia

FACT FILE

PEOPLE.................Thais
POPULATION ....about 64 million
MAIN LANGUAGE ......Thai
CAPITAL CITY.........Bangkok
MONEY.................Baht
HIGHEST MOUNTAIN ..Doi Inthanon—8,514 feet
LONGEST RIVER.......Mekong River—2,600 miles

Theater

see also: Drama, Opera

A theater is a building or place to see plays, operas, and ballets. Long ago, theaters were outdoors. They were open to the weather.

Types of theater

The first known theaters in Europe were in Greece in 600 B.C. They were outdoor theaters called amphitheaters. Today in some indoor theaters, people sit facing the performance. Movie theaters are like this. In other theaters, people sit or stand all around the stage. This is sometimes called theater-in-the-round. School auditoriums or gymnasiums can be used as theaters, too.

Performances were held outside in this ancient Greek theater. The audience sat on raised seats in a big half circle.

This is the Globe Theater in London, England. It is a copy of the old Globe Theater built 400 years ago.

Tiger

see also: Cat, Mammal

Tigers are mammals. They are the largest and strongest members of the cat family. Tigers live in forests in Asia.

Tiger families

A male is called a tiger. A female is called a tigress. A tigress will have as many as three cubs at a time. The cubs will leave their mother when they are two to three years old. Each young tiger will find a part of the forest where they will live and hunt on their own.

TIGER FACTS

NUMBER OF KINDS...	8
COLOR	golden-orange with black stripes
LENGTH	up to 10 feet
WEIGHT	up to 595 lbs.
STATUS	endangered
LIFE SPAN	15 to 20 years
ENEMIES	people

a tiger

razor-sharp teeth for killing and eating meat

long tail for balance

striped fur for moving through the trees without being seen

sharp claws for climbing and for tearing food apart

strong legs and body for running and pulling down victims

Tigers groom themselves and their cubs just as other members of the cat family do.

MEAT EATER

Tigers are patient and silent when they hunt. They follow their victims for great distances. They will hunt and eat most mammals in their territory.

Time

see also: Calendar, Measurement, Season

Time is the way people measure the periods between events. Some ways of counting time are natural. Day and night and seasons are natural time. Other ways of recording time have been invented by people. These ways fit in with nature's time.

Measuring time

There are different units of time. Something that happens slowly can be measured in years. Growing from a child to an adult is measured in years. Something that happens quickly can be measured in seconds. A blink of an eye or a sneeze can be measured in seconds.

Clocks measure time from day to day. The first clocks were sundials. They cast a shadow onto their face as the sun moves across the sky. The sundial doesn't work when the sun isn't shining. Clocks have become more and more accurate since the 1200s. Today, most clocks are electronic. The best clocks are atomic clocks. They are so good that they only lose one second of time every thousand years.

DID YOU KNOW?

The earth is divided up into 24 time zones. When it is twelve noon in one place, it is twelve midnight on the other side of the world.

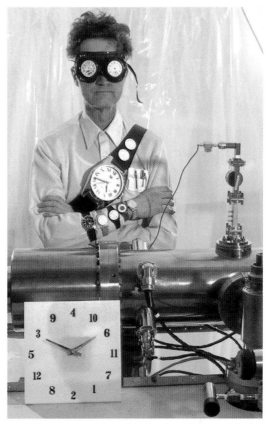

The atomic clock in the middle of the photograph is the most accurate type of clock. The scientist is wearing many other watches that are not as correct.

The shadow on this sundial says the time is ten-thirty.

Toad

see also: Amphibian, Frog, Metamorphosis

A toad is an amphibian. It is born in the water. It lives on land when it is an adult. Toads have rough, spotty skin. They have short tongues. Some toads have poisonous skin. Toads live almost everywhere in the world except in the very coldest places.

Toad families

Most toads live on their own. They come together to mate. Toads spend the daytime hiding under stones or in burrows. Female toads lay eggs in lakes or ponds. The eggs hatch into tadpoles. The tadpoles will lose their tails and grow legs. Then they are called toadlets.

TOAD FACTS

NUMBER OF KINDS	235
COLOR	green or brown
LENGTH	up to 9 inches
WEIGHT	up to 3 lbs.
STATUS	common
LIFE SPAN	about 5 years
ENEMIES	birds, snakes, fish

rough, tough skin for protection

eyes on the top of the head to look out of the water

strong legs for jumping

an American toad

PLANT, INSECT, AND MEAT EATER

A toad tadpole eats water plants and water insects. An adult toad hunts at night for insects and worms. Some kinds of big toads will even eat small snakes and birds.

Toad eggs are laid in strings. They are called toadspawn.

Tooth

see also: Human Body

Teeth are used by humans and other animals to bite and chew food. Humans and most animals do not grow new teeth if their teeth fall out or get damaged.

Kinds of teeth

Animals' teeth have special jobs for the food they eat. Most animals have three types of teeth. At the front are incisors. These snip and cut up food. To the side of the incisors are the canines. The canines are long, sharp teeth. Carnivores eat raw meat. They use the big canine teeth to hold their prey and tear off meat. Molars are the flatter teeth at the back of the mouth. They are used for grinding. Herbivores eat plants. They have wide, flat molars to grind up plants.

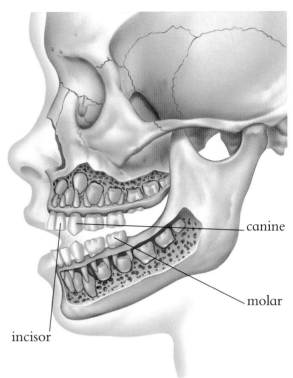

This shows the mouth of a child who still has baby teeth. The adult teeth are inside waiting to push through the gums.

Human teeth

When human beings are babies, a set of small teeth comes through the gums. These are called baby teeth. These teeth begin to fall out as the permanent or adult teeth come through the gums. Adult teeth have to last for the rest of a person's life.

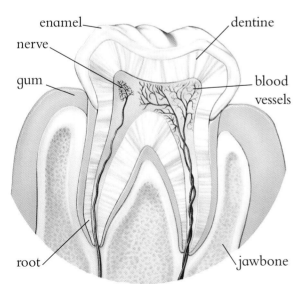

a human tooth

DID YOU KNOW?

Bacteria in the mouth make acids. The acids eat away at tooth enamel. This is called tooth decay. Brushing teeth and gums gets rid of bits of food and bacteria. A dentist can fill the holes in decaying teeth, but fillings do not last as well as enamel.

Tornado

see also: Hurricane, Weather

A tornado is a very powerful type of storm. The air twists around at very high speed. The air can move at speeds of more than 200 miles per hour. A tornado is also sometimes called a twister.

The funnel cloud of this tornado is reaching down toward the ground.

How a tornado starts

A tornado is shaped like a narrow, twisting funnel. It is made from clouds and dust. The tornado stretches from the sky down to the ground. It can move across the land. It may last for a few hours or only a few minutes.

Tornadoes begin to form over land when air starts to rise quickly. Some tornadoes begin over the sea. They are called waterspouts.

People and tornadoes

A tornado can wreck buildings, cars, and roads. The damage can be terrible. Weather forecasters try to warn people, but it is hard to know where tornadoes will go and how fast they will move. The safest place to be when a tornado strikes is in an underground shelter.

DID YOU KNOW?

There are so many tornadoes in the flat, central plains of North America that the area is called "tornado alley."

A tornado has completely destroyed this house.

Tortoise

see also: Reptile, Turtle

A tortoise is a reptile. It has a hard shell. A tortoise can pull itself inside its shell for shelter or protection. There are several kinds of tortoises in the world. Most live in hot countries. Giant tortoises live on some islands.

TORTOISE FACTS

NUMBER OF KINDS	40
COLOR	brown
LENGTH	up to 5 feet
WEIGHT	up to 540 lbs.
STATUS	some are threatened
LIFE SPAN	up to 200 years
ENEMIES	rats, cats, dogs, crabs, and birds eat baby tortoises

Tortoise families

Adult tortoises do not look after their baby tortoises. The female lays 10 to 20 round eggs. She buries them in sand or soil. The heat of the sun keeps them warm. The babies have to take care of themselves after they hatch.

It can take many years for the babies to grow into full-size tortoises.

a giant tortoise

shell to protect against enemies

claws for digging

beak for biting into food

strong, scaly legs for walking

PLANT AND MEAT EATER

Plant leaves and shoots are a tortoise's favorite food, but a tortoise will eat almost any kind of food. It will even eat dead animals.

The desert tortoise eats when there has been rain and the plants grow quickly.

Touch

see also: Smell, Taste

Touch is one of the senses. It tells human beings and animals about the things that surround them. Skin is the part of the body that is sensitive to touch.

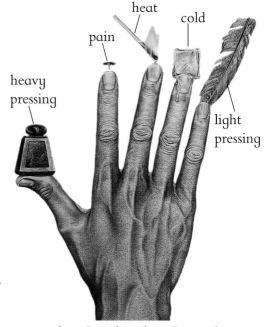

the five kinds of touch

heat

cold

pain

light pressing

heavy pressing

The five kinds of touch
The skin is sensitive to five kinds of touch. They are pain, heat, cold, heavy pressing, and light pressing. Nerves are pathways in the body. The nerves carry messages about touch to the brain. Special sense cells take feelings of touch to the nerves. The fingertips and the lips have the most of these special sense cells.

Using touch
People who cannot see clearly can use their sense of touch. Touch helps them read using Braille. People can "read" Braille with the sensitive skin of their fingertips.

Animals that live in the dark can have a very good sense of touch. Fish that live in dark or muddy water have feelers called barbels. Catfish have barbels. The barbels hang under the fish's mouth. The fish can feel things below it.

The tiny dots of Braille make letters. This lets people read with their sense of touch.

DID YOU KNOW?

Many animals have whiskers. Whiskers are long, sensitive hairs. They help animals move around in the dark. Whiskers help animals decide whether an opening is wide enough to get through or not.

Train

see also: Railroad, Transportation,

A train is a powerful machine. It runs on railroad tracks. Trains take people or goods from one place to another.

The first trains

The first trains were built more than 200 years ago. They had steam engines. A train in 1829 could go 30 miles per hour. This was faster than anyone had ever gone. Today trains are powered by diesel engines or electricity. They can travel up to 320 miles per hour.

People and trains

Trains are good at quickly carrying lots of people and goods. Underground trains are used in cities everywhere in the world.

TRAIN FACTS

FIRST TRAIN	1804, U.K.
FASTEST STEAM TRAIN	1938, U.K.–125 mph
BIGGEST ENGINE	1940s, U.S.A.–588 tons
FASTEST TRAIN	1990, France–320 mph

Trains in France can go as fast as 320 miles per hour. These trains hold the world speed record for trains.

The first passenger steam trains had open-sided passenger cars.

Transportation

see also: Railroad, Road, Waterway

Transportation is the way that people or goods are moved from place to place. Trains, cars, and horse carts are all forms of transportation.

The first transportation

Thousands of years ago, people carried everything themselves. People were the transportation. Then people trained donkeys and horses to carry things for them. They used boats to travel on water. The invention of the wheel made it easier for people and animals to carry heavy loads.

Transportation today

Today there are powerful engines for cars, trains, boats, and airplanes. People can fly long distances in a few hours.

Transportation has not changed much in areas of the world where there are few cars. People still walk, ride bicycles, and use animals to carry things.

TRANSPORTATION FIRSTS

FIRST BOATS	prehistoric times
FIRST WHEELED CARTS	3500 B.C.
FIRST HORSE-DRAWN BUS	1662
FIRST STEAMSHIPS	1783
FIRST STEAM TRAIN	1804
FIRST CARS	1885
FIRST AIRPLANES	1903

People could travel by bicycle, bus, or automobile in the 1890s.

DID YOU KNOW?

Someone who travels on a form of transportation is called a passenger. People who travel from home to work are called commuters.

Modern transportation can travel fast. Too much traffic can slow things down.

Tree

see also: Forest, Rain Forest, Wood

Trees are the largest plants. Broadleafed trees have broad, flat leaves. Conifers have thin, needlelike leaves. Most conifers are called evergreens because they have green leaves all year round. Trees in cold places lose their leaves in the autumn.

bark protects the living wood

leaves take in light, carbon dioxide, and water

an English oak

trunk holds the tree up and carries water and minerals to the leaves and branches

The life of a tree

Most trees grow from seeds which have fallen onto the ground. A young tree is called a seedling until it is about as tall as an adult person. Then the young tree is called a sapling. Many trees growing together are called a wood or a forest. Trees can grow in most places on land. They do not grow where it is very cold, dry, or windy.

People use trees in many ways. Some trees produce fruits or nuts. Other trees produce rubber, cork, and wood gums. Wood from trees is used in buildings and to make furniture, toys, and paper.

DID YOU KNOW?

The tallest trees are the Giant Sequoias. They can grow to more than 360 feet tall.

This woman in Sri Lanka is a rubber tapper. She collects sap from the tree to make rubber.

Triceratops

see also: Dinosaur, Fossil

The triceratops was a big,
three-horned dinosaur. It had
a heavy, bony head. Its head
was the length of a tall man.
A triceratops weighed as much
as an elephant. The triceratops
lived 65 million years ago.
It was one of the
last dinosaurs.

TRICERATOPS FACTS

COLOR	not known
LENGTH	30 feet
WEIGHT	about 6 tons
FIRST FOSSILS FOUND	1880s–U.S.A.

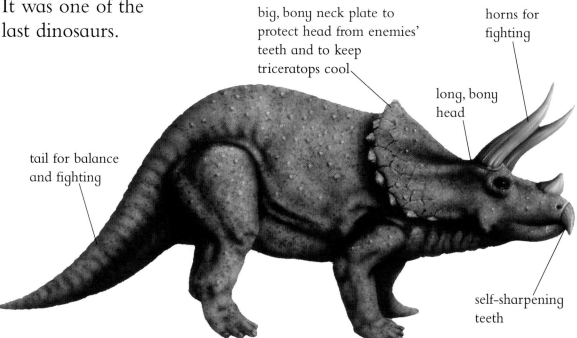

big, bony neck plate to
protect head from enemies'
teeth and to keep
triceratops cool

horns for
fighting

long, bony
head

tail for balance
and fighting

self-sharpening
teeth

triceratops

Lifestyle

There were many kinds of
triceratops. They lived in groups or
herds. They ate low-growing plants.
Their horns and giant heads were
used for fighting off attackers
such as tyrannosaurus.

PLANT EATER

*Triceratops ate low branches and
leaves. It had self-sharpening teeth.
As triceratops chewed, each tooth
wore down to a new, sharp edge.*

Trinidad and Tobago

see also: South America

Trinidad and Tobago are islands in the Caribbean Sea. Trinidad is crossed by three rows of hills. It has swamps in the east and west. Tobago is low land. Its mountains in the east are covered in forests. Both islands have hot summers and warm winters.

These Tobagonian workers are making umbrellas to shade the people on the beach.

Living in Trinidad and Tobago

More than half the people live in cities. There are mines and factories. Lots of oil is produced. Farmers grow sugar cane, cocoa, coffee, coconuts, citrus fruits, and rice. Fishing is an important industry.

The ancestors of Trinidadians and Tobagonians came from Africa, Asia, and South America.

DID YOU KNOW?

Trinidad holds a carnival in the city of Port-of-Spain. People wear fantastic costumes. They sing calypso music and play oil drum instruments in steel bands.

People from other countries go to Trinidad and Tobago for vacations. They enjoy the spicy food, beautiful beaches, and calypso music.

South America

FACT FILE

PEOPLE	Trinidadians, Tobagonians
POPULATION	about 1 million
MAIN LANGUAGES	English, Spanish, Hindi
CAPITAL CITY	Port-of-Spain
MONEY	Trinidad and Tobago dollar
HIGHEST MOUNTAIN	Cerro Aripo–3,085 feet
LONGEST RIVER	Ortoire River–31 miles

Truck

see also: Road, Transportation

A truck is a large, heavy vehicle. It is used for carrying goods on roads. Most trucks can have as many as eighteen wheels. The place where the driver sits in front is called a cab. In some places in the world, trucks are called lorries.

The first trucks

The first trucks were built a hundred years ago. They were powered by steam or electric engines. Then diesel engines were invented. Now most trucks are powered by diesel.

People and trucks

Trucks can pull very heavy loads. Trucks carry almost everything people buy and use. Trucks carry large boxes or containers to and from factories, farms, shipping ports, and railroads.

Many trucks have special uses. Refrigerated trucks, fire engines, garbage trucks, and tow trucks are all special trucks.

This 1921 delivery truck has a gasoline engine. Some deliveries at this time were still made with horse-drawn carts.

Huge trucks like this are sometimes called 18-wheelers.

Tubman, Harriet

see also: Slavery

Harriet Tubman was a person who fought against slavery. She helped many slaves to escape.

Slavery and escape

Tubman was born a slave in Maryland around 1820. Her parents were slaves, too. Tubman's large family lived in one small room with no furniture.

Tubman had to start work when she was very small. Tubman wanted to escape. In 1849, she escaped with the help of local white people. They were part of the "Underground Railroad." Tubman was taken from house to house. The houses were the "stations" of the "railroad." Tubman reached Pennsylvania, where there was no slavery.

Tubman was sometimes called "Moses" because she led people to freedom.

Helping others to freedom

Tubman became a "conductor" on the Underground Railroad. She helped more than 300 people to reach freedom.

During the Civil War, Tubman was a nurse, a cook, a scout, and a spy. After slavery ended, Tubman campaigned for women's rights. In 1908 she made a home for old people. She helped start schools for African-American children. She died in 1913.

This painting shows people working for the Underground Railroad. They are leading a group of runaway slaves to freedom. The farm in the painting was owned by anti-slavery campaigners.

DID YOU KNOW?

The Underground Railroad was at its largest from 1830 to 1860. It helped thousands of slaves escape from states in the South. It took them to northern states or to Canada.

Tundra

see also: Arctic

Tundra is the name given to the very cold places along the Arctic Circle. There is tundra in the north of Asia, Europe, and North America.

Tundra weather

The temperature in the tundra is below freezing for most of the year. It can get as cold as −104°F in winter. Only in summer does the temperature get just above freezing at 32°F. It is usually very dry in the tundra, but it does snow there.

Life in the tundra

Some animals move south when the tundra is frozen in the winter. Other animals hibernate. They do not come out again until the summer. The top layers of soil thaw in summer. The ground becomes marshy. Then small plants grow. Some of these plants are mosses, lichens, and short grasses. Herds of musk oxen, caribou, and reindeer go to the tundra to graze. Smaller animals, such as lemmings, rabbits, foxes, and swarms of mosquitoes, live there, too.

Few people live in the tundra, but the Inuit of North America and the Lapps of Scandinavia have lived there for a long time.

This Lapp family lives in the tundra areas in the summer.

DID YOU KNOW?

High, flat areas in mountains can have a kind of tundra. This area is called an alpine tundra.

Some tundra areas turn green during the short summer.

Tunisia

see also: Africa

Tunisia is a country in northern Africa. There are mountains in the northwest. Hills are in the southeast. Tunisia has lowland areas with salt lakes. The coast has good farm land. The south is dry and hot. The north is wet and warm.

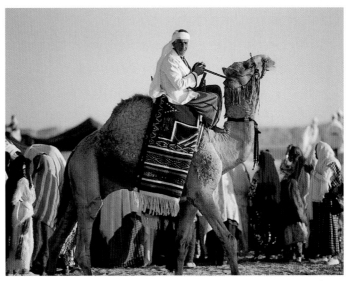

Some people travel by camel in parts of Tunisia. Woven rugs with bright patterns cover the camels' backs.

Living in Tunisia

Many people live in cities along the coasts. There are mines and factories. Farmers grow fruit, dates, and olives. Tunisians eat a semolina cake. It is made with crushed dates and honey. The people keep herds of sheep, goats, cattle, and camels.

Many tourists enjoy the sunny beaches. They shop in the busy markets. Fine leatherwork and silk carpets are made in Tunisia.

DID YOU KNOW?

The city of Tunis is built near the ruins of the ancient city of Carthage. Carthage was the center of a great empire about 2,100 years ago.

Africa

FACT FILE

PEOPLE	Tunisians
POPULATION	almost 10 million
MAIN LANGUAGES	Arabic, French
CAPITAL CITY	Tunis
MONEY	Tunisian dinar
HIGHEST MOUNTAIN	Jeb el Chambi–5,067 feet
LONGEST RIVER	Majardah River–224 miles

Turkey

see also: Asia, Europe

Turkey is a country in the Middle East. The biggest part of Turkey is in Asia. A small part of Turkey is in Europe. The weather is mild and wet in winter. It is hot and dry in summer. It snows in the mountains in the winter.

Living in Turkey

Just less than half of the people work on farms. Farmers raise sheep. They grow figs and cotton. The cotton is used to make cloth and goods such as rugs. These goods are made in factories.

Tourists go to Turkey to enjoy the beaches and good weather. They also visit the ancient ruins.

Lamb is often cooked over an open fire. Food is sometimes wrapped in vine leaves. Turks drink small cups of strong Turkish coffee.

The huge covered market in Istanbul sells everything from brassware to olives.

DID YOU KNOW?

Mount Ararat in Turkey is said to be the place where Noah's Ark came to rest after a great flood. This story is in the Bible.

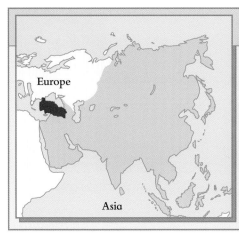

Europe

Asia

FACT FILE

PEOPLE	Turks, Turkish
POPULATION	almost 69 million
MAIN LANGUAGE	Turkish
CAPITAL CITY	Ankara
BIGGEST CITY	Istanbul
MONEY	Turkish lira
HIGHEST MOUNTAIN	Mount Ararat—16,951 feet
LONGEST RIVER	Kizl Irmak—714 miles